Understanding Cat Behavior and Training for Good Behavior

© Copyright 2023 - All rights reserved.

You may not reproduce, duplicate or send the contents of this book without direct written permission from the author. You cannot hereby despite any circumstance blame the publisher or hold him or her to legal responsibility for any reparation, compensations, or monetary forfeiture owing to the information included herein, either in a direct or an indirect way.

Legal Notice: This book has copyright protection. You can use the book for personal purposes. You should not sell, use, alter, distribute, quote, take excerpts, or paraphrase in part or whole the material contained in this book without obtaining the permission of the author first.

Disclaimer Notice: You must take note that the information in this document is for casual reading and entertainment purposes only. We have made every attempt to provide accurate, up-to-date, and reliable information. We do not express or imply guarantees of any kind. The persons who read admit that the writer is not occupied in giving legal, financial, medical, or other advice. We put this book content by sourcing various places.

Please consult a licensed professional before you try any techniques shown in this book. By going through this document, the book lover comes to an agreement that under no situation is the author accountable for any forfeiture, direct or indirect, which they may incur because of the use of material contained in this document, including, but not limited to, α errors, comissions, or inaccuracies.

Chapters

Decoding Feline Behavior..................4

Understanding the Feline Mind..................8

Reading Your Cat's Body Language..................11

The Vocal Language of Cats..................14

Feline Communication..................17

The Importance of Play for Cats..................20

Cat Behavior Problems..................23

Socializing Your Kitten..................26

Building a Strong Bond with Your Cat..................29

Positive Reinforcement Training for Cats..................32

Teaching Your Cat Tricks..................35

Environmental Enrichment for Cats..................38

Managing Cat Territorial Behavior..................42

Dealing with Cat Anxiety..................46

Indoor vs. Outdoor Cats..................50

Introducing Your Cat to Other Pets..................54

Nutrition and Feline Behavior..................58

Cat Breeds and Personalities..................61

Senior Cat Care..................64

Maintaining Good Behavior..................68

Decoding Feline Behavior

Cats are fascinating creatures with individual personalities, quirks, and behaviors. As a cat parent, decoding your feline friend's behavior is essential for creating a strong bond and providing them with the best care possible. In this chapter, we'll look at some of the most common behaviors displayed by cats and what they signify.

Body Language

One of the best ways to communicate with your cat is through body language. Cats use their bodies to express a variety of emotions, from fear and aggression to joy and relaxation. As a cat parent, it's essential for you to learn how to read your cat's body language in order to better comprehend its needs and feelings.

Here are some common body language cues to watch out for:

Ears: A cat's ears can be an excellent indicator of its mood. When they're feeling contented and relaxed, their ears will be upright facing forward. Conversely, if their ears are flattened against their head, then it could indicate fear or defensiveness.

Tail: A cat's position of its tail can give insight into its mood. If it is held high and puffed up, this indicates they feel threatened or aggressive; on the other hand, a relaxed tail indicates contentment and contentment.

Eyes: Cat's eyes can convey a great deal about its emotional state. Dilated pupils indicate anxiety or fear, while narrowed pupils suggest anger or aggression.

Vocalizations

Cats are known for their wide array of vocalizations, from soft meows to loud yowls. Understanding what your cat's vocalizations signify can help you better comprehend their behavior.

Here are some common vocalizations and what they signify:

Meows: Cats use meows primarily to communicate with humans, rather than other cats. A short, high-pitched meow may indicate a greeting while an extended low-pitched meow may signify distress or require attention.

Purrs: Cats often purr when they're content or contented, but they may also purr when feeling anxious or in pain.

Hisses and Growls: These sounds can be indicative of a cat feeling threatened or defensive.

Behavioral Issues

Understanding your cat's behavior is essential for addressing any behavioral problems it may be displaying. Common behaviors include scratching furniture, aggression, and litter box issues. By understanding the underlying causes of these behaviors, you can take steps to modify them and prevent them from becoming long-term issues.

For instance, scratching furniture is an instinctive behavior for cats but can be frustrating for owners. To help redirect their behavior, providing your cat with a scratch post or pad and teaching them to use it are two methods that may work: aggression indicates stress or fear and can indicate triggers that cause aggression in cats; identifying these triggers and taking steps to address them effectively will help solve the issue at hand.

Conclusion

Decoding your cat's behavior requires patience, observation, and an acute sense of empathy. By learning to read your feline friend's body language, vocalizations, and behavioral cues, you can develop a deeper connection with them and provide them with the best care possible. Remember that cats are complex creatures with unique personalities - so take time to get to know each one individually!

Understanding the Feline Mind

Cats have long been renowned for their mysterious and enigmatic nature. As cat owners, it can be difficult to comprehend why our feline friends behave the way they do. But by taking a closer look into the feline mind, we can gain a better insight into what drives cats so incredibly differently.

Understanding Feline Psychology | Understanding the Basics

Cat behavior is fundamentally driven by instincts and reflexes, making them prime candidates to study the feline mind. Knowing these drives helps us better comprehend why cats act the way they do - as natural predators with hardwired drives to hunt and kill prey.

Cats possess an instinctive territorial behavior that can be highly protective. Cats mark their territory with scent and behavior, marking it off from other cats or even humans if they feel their territory is being threatened. This instinctive drive may lead to conflict with other cats or even humans if a cat feels their territory is being invaded.

Feline psychology also involves social behavior. Cats are highly social creatures, though not always, in the same way, dogs or humans do. While some cats are more outgoing than others, most form strong bonds with their owners and may become attached to certain objects or places within their homes.

Cats possess an inquisitive spirit and enjoy exploring their environment. They're proficient at problem-solving and can be taught various tasks such as hunting and retrieving or using a litter box.

How Cats Learn

Understanding how cats learn is essential to comprehending the feline mind. Cats are intelligent creatures capable of learning through observation, trial, and error, as well as reinforcement.

One of the most successful methods for training cats is positive reinforcement. This involves rewarding your cat for good behavior with treats, praise, or affection. Over time, your feline friend will learn that certain behaviors lead to positive outcomes and be more likely to repeat those same actions in the future.

Cats possess excellent memory, which allows them to retain people, places, and events from years ago. This explains why cats often manage to find their way home after being lost for an extended period of time.

Conclusion

Gaining insight into the feline mind is a complex and ongoing process, but it's an essential part of being an attentive cat parent. By understanding cat instincts, behaviors, and learning capabilities we can give our furry friends all of the love and care they require to live happy, healthy lives. Remember to be patient as each cat is unique with their own personality traits and preferences - take time to get to know your feline friend on an individual level for best results!

Reading Your Cat's Body Language

Cats are highly social creatures and often express their emotions through body language. Learning how to read your cat's body language can help you better comprehend their needs and feelings. In this chapter, we'll look at some of the most common signs cats give off and interpret what they signify.

Ears

Cat's ears are among the most expressive parts of its body. When alert and interested in what's around them, their ears will be perked up and face forward. Conversely, if their ears are flattened against their head it could indicate fear or defensiveness; similarly, if one ear is facing forward while the other remains flattened it may indicate conflicted emotions within a cat.

Tail

A cat's position of its tail can provide insight into its mood. When their tail is held high and puffed up, it could indicate they feel threatened or aggressive; conversely, if their tail is held low and relaxed, then this usually implies they are feeling contented and contented.

Cats can communicate with their tails in various ways. If a cat's tail is wagging rapidly, it may indicate that they're feeling anxious or frustrated. On the other hand, the slow, gentle swishing of the tail could indicate that a cat is feeling relaxed and contented.

Eyes

A cat's eyes can tell us a great deal about its emotions. If the pupils of an indoor cat are dilated, that indicates anxiety or fear; conversely, constricted pupils indicate calm and relaxation.

Cat's eyes can convey affection and trust. If your feline friend is slowly blinking at you, it's a sign that they feel safe in your presence - this behavior is commonly referred to as a "cat kiss," signifying love and devotion.

Body Posture

Cats use their bodies to express a variety of emotions, from fear and aggression to happiness and relaxation.

When feeling threatened or defensive, cats may arch their back and puff up their fur in an effort to appear larger and more intimidating. On the other hand, when feeling relaxed and contented, cats may lie on their side or back with their legs stretched out.

One important aspect of body posture to observe is your cat's stance. If they appear to be standing with their weight shifted forward and muscles tense, it could indicate they're feeling aggressive or defensive. On the contrary, if their feet are shifted back and muscles relaxed, then it suggests they are feeling calm and contented.

Conclusion

Reading your cat's body language is an integral part of being a responsible cat parent. By understanding your feline friend's ears, tail, eyes, and overall posture you can better comprehend their needs and emotions. Remember that every cat is unique so take the time to get to know them on an individual level with patience and observation. With patience and attentiveness, you will gain a better insight into their behavior as well as form a life-long bond with them.

The Vocal Language of Cats

Cats are known for their variety of vocalizations, from soft meows to loud yowls. As a responsible cat parent, it's important to understand your cat's vocalizations and what they signify. In this chapter, we'll look at some common vocalizations and explain what they signify.

Meows

Cats often use meows to communicate with humans more than other cats. A short, high-pitched meow could signify a greeting or request for attention; on the other hand, an extended low-pitched meow could indicate distress or require extra care.

Some cats are more vocal than others, and some breeds, like Siamese cats, are known for their loud, persistent meows. If your cat's meowing is excessive, it is essential to rule out any medical issues and give them the love and attention that they require.

Purrs

Cats often purr when they're feeling content or happy. Purring can also occur when cats experience anxiety or pain. Purring is a complex behavior involving muscle contractions and breathing. Some experts speculate that purring may have therapeutic benefits for cats, helping to calm them down and reduce stress levels.

Hisses and Growls

Hissing and growling are defensive vocalizations cats use when feeling threatened or scared. These sounds usually accompany aggressive body languages like arched backs or puffed-up fur.

If your cat is hissing or growling at you, it is essential to give them space and avoid approaching until they have calmed down. Furthermore, try to identify what might be causing their fear or anxiety and address it if possible.

Chirps and Trills

Chirps and trills are soft, bird-like sounds cats make to communicate with other cats and sometimes humans.

These noises may be used as a greeting or sign of affection.

When your cat starts chirping or trilling at you, it's a sign that they're feeling contented in your company. Reacting to their noises can help deepen the bond between you and your furry friend.

Conclusion

Understanding cats' vocal language is an integral part of being a responsible cat parent. By understanding your cat's vocalizations, you can better comprehend their needs and emotions. Remember, every cat is unique, so take time to get to know your furry friend on an individual level through patience and observation. With patience and persistence, you will develop an intimate bond with your feline friend that will last throughout life.

Feline Communication

Cats are highly social creatures that use various communication methods to interact with each other and humans. Understanding feline communication is an essential part of being a responsible cat parent, so in this chapter, we'll take a look at some of the most frequent communication techniques cats employ and what it means.

Scent Marking

Cats utilize scent marking as one of their primary communication methods. Cats possess scent glands located throughout their bodies, which they use to leave marks on objects and surfaces around them. Scent marking helps cats establish territory and communicate with other cats nearby.

Common behaviors seen with cats when scent-marking include rubbing their faces and bodies against objects and surfaces, scratching with paws, and urinating on these same objects and surfaces. If your feline friend is marking in your home, provide them with appropriate outlets such as scratching posts and litter boxes for this behavior.

Visual Cues

Cats use a variety of visual cues to communicate with other cats and humans. As we've previously seen, a cat's body language can reveal important information about its moods and emotions. Other visible elements that cats use include their eyes, ears, and tails.

For instance, when your cat is feeling relaxed and contented, it may close its eyes or even fall asleep. On the other hand, if they're feeling agitated or defensive, their eyes may open wide with dilated pupils. Paying attention to your cat's visual cues can help you better comprehend its needs and emotions.

Vocalizations

As previously discussed in Chapter 4, cats use a variety of vocalizations to communicate with other cats and humans. Meows, purrs, hisses, and growls are just some of the sounds these felines can make.

Cats use vocalizations to establish social hierarchies and convey their intentions to other cats. For instance, a dominant cat may use an aggressive meow in order to intimidate a subordinate cat; on the other hand, a submissive cat may use a soft, gentle meow as a signal that they are willing to cooperate.

Conclusion

Feline communication is an intricate and fascinating topic that's essential to comprehending and caring for our feline friends. By understanding the different methods cats use to express themselves, we can better comprehend their needs and emotions. Remember, each cat is unique; take time to get to know your pal on an individual level through patience and observation. Doing this will give you a deeper insight into your furry friend's behavior as well as foster a lifelong bond between both of you.

The Importance of Play for Cats

Play is an integral part of a cat's physical and psychological well-being. As natural predators, cats require activities that simulate hunting and stalking to remain healthy and content. In this chapter, we'll look into why play is so important for cats and how best to give your furry friend mental stimulation.

Physical Benefits of Play

Playing provides cats with numerous physical advantages, such as exercise and stress relief. Regular play sessions can help your cat maintain a healthy weight, build muscle tone, and reduce the likelihood of obesity-related health issues.

Play also gives cats an outlet for their energy and helps relieve stress and anxiety. Without play, cats may become bored and lethargic, leading to behavioral issues like aggression or destructive behavior.

Mental Benefits of Play

In addition to physical benefits, play provides cats with important mental stimulation. Play can reduce boredom and prevent depression in cats, which could otherwise lead to various health issues.

Playing with a cat helps to stimulate its natural instincts and encourages hunting and stalking behavior, which could reduce the likelihood of destructive behavior like scratching furniture or curtains.

Cats Need Variety and Purpose when Playing

Cats benefit from a variety of types of play, including interactive play with their owners, solo play with toys, and even playtime with other cats.

Interacting with your cat through interactive play is one of the best ways to give them physical and mental stimulation. Toys such as wands or laser pointers can help simulate hunting and stalking behavior while giving your feline an outlet for its energy.

Solo play with toys is essential for cats. Providing your cat with various toys like catnip toys, balls, and puzzles helps them remain entertained and engaged even when you're not present.

Playing with other cats can be beneficial for cats, as it provides them with social interaction and stimulates their natural instincts. If you have more than one cat, providing them with opportunities to play together will help strengthen their bond and reduce conflict chances.

Conclusion

Play is an integral part of your cat's physical and mental well-being. By giving them regular opportunities to play, you can help maintain their health, happiness, and engagement. Be sure to provide various toys and activities tailored to each cat's individual needs and preferences. With patience and love, you can build a strong bond with your furry friend through playtime.

Cat Behavior Problems

No matter how much we adore our feline friends, they may sometimes display behavior issues that can be frustrating or even harmful. As responsible cat parents, it is essential to recognize the causes of these issues and take steps to address them. In this chapter, we'll look at some of the most common cat behavior issues and provide solutions on how you can address them.

Litter Box Problems

Litter box issues are a common behavioral issue among cats. Some cats may refuse to use the litter box, while others use it inconsistently or inappropriately. There can be various reasons why your feline friend may experience litter box issues, such as medical issues, stress, and an aversion to using the box itself.

If your cat is having litter box issues, it's essential to first rule out any medical causes. Once these have been addressed, you can begin addressing the underlying cause of the issue by providing them with a clean and accessible litter box, using appropriate litter, and alleviating stress or anxiety in their environment. These steps may help address litter box problems once and for all.

Scratching and Destructive Behavior

Cats have the natural urge to scratch, and this behavior can become destructive when they scratch furniture or other objects in the home. This type of behavior often stems from boredom, stress, or lack of appropriate scratching surfaces.

Provide your cat with a variety of scratching surfaces, such as scratching posts and mats, to redirect their clawing away from furniture and other objects. It is also essential to address any underlying stress or anxiety in their environment and offer them plenty of opportunities for play and stimulation.

Aggression

Cats' aggression can be caused by a variety of reasons, such as fear, territorial behavior, and past experiences. Aggressive behaviors in cats may include biting, scratching, and hissing and may be directed toward other cats, humans, or both.

If your cat is displaying aggressive behavior, it's essential to identify and address its underlying cause and address it appropriately. This may involve providing them with more socialization opportunities, managing any territorial behavior issues, and seeking professional help from a veterinarian or animal behaviorist.

Conclusion

Cat behavior problems can be challenging for cat parents, but they are usually manageable with the right approach. By understanding and addressing the causes of these issues, you can help your feline friend lead a happier and healthier life. Remember that each cat is unique; take time to get to know them on an individual level by showing patience, understanding, and attention; this will help build a strong bond between you both while helping solve any behavioral issues they may have.

Socializing Your Kitten

Socializing your kitten is an integral part of raising a happy and healthy cat. Kittens that have been socialized are more likely to feel secure around other cats, humans, and new experiences. In this chapter, we'll cover the significance of socializing your kitten as well as some effective methods for doing so.

Why Socializing Your Kitten Is Important

Why does socializing your kitten matter so much?

Kittens who haven't been socialized properly may become fearful or aggressive toward other cats, humans, and new experiences. This may lead to behavior problems like scratching, biting, and avoiding social interaction. With proper socialization, your kitten will learn how to be comfortable around people, other animals, and new environments.

Socializing your kitten early on can help to prevent behavioral issues in later life. Socialized kittens tend to be less fearful of new experiences and tend to be confident and well-adjusted cats.

Socializing Your Kitten

When socializing your kitten, the ideal period is between three and fourteen weeks old. At this age, kittens are more open to new experiences and more willing to engage in interactions.

One of the best ways to socialize your kitten is by exposing them to a variety of people, animals, and environments. Invite friends and family members to interact with your kitten, giving them chances to meet other cats and animals in a controlled setting.

It is essential to provide your kitten with a variety of toys and play experiences so they can learn and develop social skills. Interactive toys such as wands or laser pointers can help simulate hunting or stalking behavior while giving your kitten something to do besides run around in.

Another effective way to socialize your kitten is by enrolling them in a kitten socialization class or playgroup. These events offer kittens a safe environment where they can interact with other cats and humans alike.

Conclusion

Socializing your kitten is an integral part of raising a happy and healthy feline. By exposing them to different people, animals, and environments, you can help them develop the social skills necessary for confident adults with excellent manners. Remember that each kitten is unique so take time to get to know your furry friend on an individual level through patience, understanding, and attention. With patience, understanding, and attention you can foster an enduring bond with your kitten that will last throughout its lifetime as a well-socialized adult cat.

Building a Strong Bond with Your Cat

Establishing a strong bond with your cat is essential for its well-being and the happiness of both parties. Fostering such understanding and patience takes time, so in this chapter, we'll look at some of the most effective methods of creating such a connection with your furry friend.

Spend Quality Time Together

One of the best ways to foster a deep bond with your cat is to spend quality time together. This could include playing, cuddling, and grooming your furry friend. Regular positive interactions will help your feline associate you with positive memories and further cement the two of you's connection.

It's essential to remember that every cat is unique and may enjoy different types of activities. Some cats enjoy engaging in interactive play with toys, while others may opt for quieter pursuits such as reading a book or watching TV with their owner. Paying attention to your cat's preferences and tailoring your interactions accordingly can help build a stronger bond between both of you.

Understanding and Respecting Your Cat's Boundaries

Spending quality time with your cat is important, but it's equally essential to respect their boundaries. Cats are independent creatures and may not always want to be held or petted. Therefore, allow them to come to you when they show interest in affection and avoid forcing interactions if they seem uncomfortable or stressed.

Providing Your Cat with a Comfy Environment

Giving your feline friend the comfort of an environment they can call their own is key to providing them with a happy life.

Provide your cat with a comfortable and secure environment to strengthen the bond between you and your feline friend. This includes providing them with access to food and water, as well as having access to an up-to-date litter box. Creating such an atmosphere makes your feline friend feel secure and contented in their home.

Communication and Understanding Communication facilitates communication and understanding when both parties are on the same page.

Communication and understanding are essential for creating a deep bond with your cat. Recognizing and reading your cat's body language and vocalizations can help you comprehend their needs and emotions better. Responding to these cues by offering them affection and providing them with the necessary attention will only strengthen this already strong connection between you two.

Conclusion

Forming a strong bond with your cat requires time, patience, and understanding. By spending quality time together, respecting their boundaries, providing them with a comfortable environment, and communicating effectively, you can foster an everlasting bond with your furry friend. Remember that each cat is unique so take the time to get to know them on an individual level through patience and attention; this will lead to deeper insight into their behavior as well as foster the development of an everlasting attachment between both of you.

Positive Reinforcement Training for Cats

Positive reinforcement training is an incredibly effective and popular method to train your cat. This method uses rewards like treats and praise as motivation to encourage desired behaviors in your feline companion. In this chapter, we'll look into the advantages of positive reinforcement training for cats and some of its best applications.

Why Positive Reinforcement Training Is Effective

Positive reinforcement training is successful because it uses rewards to motivate your cat to exhibit desired behaviors. This method of instruction works on the assumption that animals will repeat behaviors that have been rewarded and avoid those which aren't.

Positive reinforcement training is an effective way to teach your cat various behaviors, such as using the litter box correctly, scratching appropriate surfaces, and even performing tricks like sitting and shaking hands. Not only that but positive reinforcement also helps build the bond between you and your feline by offering positive experiences for both of you.

Effective Positive Reinforcement Training Strategies

Positive reinforcement training requires using rewards your cat finds valuable. This could include treats, praise, and playtime. Furthermore, it's essential to give rewards immediately after your cat exhibits the desired behavior as this helps them make the connection between their reward and behavior.

Start positive reinforcement training your cat by recognizing the behavior you want them to reward and selecting a treat or playtime they value after using their scratching post. For instance, if you want them to use their scratching post more frequently, offer them either treat or playtime immediately after they do so.

It is essential to be patient and consistent when using positive reinforcement training on your cat. It may take some time for them to learn the desired behavior, so it's essential that you remain patient and provide constant positive reinforcement.

When training your cat, avoid using punishment or negative reinforcement. Doing so can cause fear and anxiety in both of you, thus damaging the relationship with your furry friend. Instead, focus on using positive reinforcement to encourage desired behaviors.

Conclusion

Positive reinforcement training is an effective and efficient way to train your cat. Utilizing rewards like treats and praise, you can motivate your feline friend to exhibit desired behaviors while strengthening the bond you share. Be patient and consistent when using positive reinforcement training - never use punishment or negative reinforcement! With patience, understanding, and attention you can foster a deep bond with your furry friend while encouraging positive behavior through this method of positive reinforcement training.

Teaching Your Cat Tricks

Teaching your cat tricks not only provides entertainment but can also strengthen the bond between you and your furry friend. Cats are intelligent animals and can learn a variety of behaviors - from basic commands to more complex ones. In this chapter, we'll look at some of the best methods for teaching your feline friend new skills.

Selecting the Appropriate Tricks

Before you start teaching your cat tricks, it is essential that you select ones suitable for their personality and abilities. Some cats may prefer simpler behaviors like sitting or shaking hands while others can learn more complex behaviors like jumping through hoops or playing fetch.

It's essential to be patient and select tricks within your cat's ability level. Additionally, rewarding your furry friend with treats, praise, or playtime for the successful completion of these tasks will bring about positive reinforcement such as increased motivation.

Utilizing Positive Reinforcement

Positive reinforcement is an effective method for teaching your cat tricks. Utilizing rewards like treats and praise, you can incentivize your feline companion to exhibit desired behaviors. Make sure they receive reinforcement immediately after demonstrating the desired behavior; this helps them make the connection between their good deed and its reward.

It is essential to be patient and consistent when providing positive reinforcement for your cat. It may take some time for them to learn the desired behavior, so be patient and keep providing rewards.

Breaking Behaviors Down Into Steps

Breaking behaviors down into steps can make it easier for your cat to learn new tricks. For instance, if you want them to jump through a hoop, start by rewarding them for standing near the hoop, then approaching it, then jumping through. This way, your feline friend will feel successful every time they succeed!

By breaking the behavior into smaller steps, you can help your cat learn the trick more quickly and with less frustration.

Conclusion

Teaching your cat tricks can be a fun and rewarding experience for both of you. By selecting appropriate tricks, using positive reinforcement, and breaking behaviors into steps, you can teach your furry friend various tricks while strengthening the bond between both of you. Remember, every cat is unique so take time to get to know them individually. With patience, understanding, and attention, you'll have no trouble teaching your new tricks while building an even closer connection.

Environmental Enrichment for Cats

Environmental enrichment is an integral part of cat care that can significantly enhance your furry friend's quality of life. Cats are intelligent and curious creatures, so providing them with a stimulating environment helps prevent behavioral issues and promotes their overall well-being. In this chapter, we'll look at some of the best methods for providing environmental enrichment to your cat.

Offering Play and Exercise Opportunities

Play and exercise opportunities for cats are essential elements of environmental enrichment. Cats need to be able to express natural behaviors such as climbing, scratching, and stalking prey; providing your feline friend with various toys, scratching posts, and climbing structures can help meet these needs while giving them something productive to do with all that energy.

Interactive play with toys like wands and laser pointers can also help simulate hunting and stalking behavior in your cat, providing it with mental stimulation.

Promoting Safe Outdoor Access

Safe outdoor access can be achieved by creating safe access points.

Though it may not always be safe or practical for cats to have outdoor access, providing them with a secure outdoor space can offer important environmental enrichment. Building an enclosure or catio can give your feline friend fresh air and an exciting environment while keeping them safe from potential dangers such as traffic or predators.

Provide Hiding and Resting Places

Offering safe havens for travelers is one of the main objectives of this project.

Cats require a range of hiding and resting places in their environment, such as cozy beds, soft blankets, and enclosed spaces like cat trees or boxes. Offering your cat various hiding and resting spots helps reduce stress levels and promote relaxation.

Constructing a Multi-Level Environment

Cats are inherently climbers and enjoy being able to access elevated areas. To give your feline friend the best environment possible in your home, create a multi-level environment with cat trees, shelves, and other elevated surfaces - including cat trees!

Offering Scent and Taste Stimulation

Cats possess an acute sense of smell, making them ideal candidates for environmental enrichment. Treating your cat to scented toys or hiding treats around the house will provide mental stimulation and encourage curiosity.

Offering a diverse menu of foods with various textures and flavors can not only offer taste stimulation but can also promote mental and physical well-being.

Conclusion

Environmental enrichment is an integral part of cat care that can enhance your feline friend's quality of life. By providing play and exercise opportunities, creating safe outdoor access, creating hiding and resting places, creating a multi-level environment, and offering scent and taste stimulation - you can help prevent behavioral problems and promote overall well-being. Remember each cat is unique so take time to get to know them on an individual level by offering patience, understanding, and affection. With these enriched environments in place, foster happiness and health throughout life for your furry pal!

Managing Cat Territorial Behavior

Cats have a strong territorial instinct, which may manifest itself in aggressive behavior towards other cats or humans if they feel their territory is being threatened. In this chapter, we'll look at effective methods for managing cat territorial behavior and maintaining peace in your home.

Understand Cat Territory with Clarity

Understanding your cat's territory is essential for managing its territorial behavior. Cats view their domain as a secure haven and may become stressed or aggressive if they feel their security is being threatened.

Cats' territories can extend far beyond their home, including outdoor space and even food and water bowls. To ensure that your feline friend feels secure and contented while living with you, it's essential that they have a secure haven of their own.

Introduce New Cats into Your Home

Are You Looking for a Way to Welcome New Kittens into Your Life?

Adopting a new cat into your home can be daunting, especially if you already have an established resident cat. To ensure a smooth introduction process for both of you, it's best to introduce them slowly and gradually, providing them with a secure space where they can interact safely and comfortably.

When welcoming new cats into your home, it's essential that each cat have its own food, water, and litter box. Doing this can prevent territorial disputes and foster a tranquil environment for everyone involved.

Providing Vertical Space

Offering vertical spaces like cat trees or shelves can help manage territorial behavior. Cats feel more secure when they have a high vantage point to observe their environment, and providing this kind of area may reduce stress and promote relaxation.

Utilizing Pheromone Products

Pheromone products, such as sprays and diffusers, can assist in managing territorial behavior in cats. These releases calming pheromones which reduce stress and promote relaxation in cats.

It's essential to note that not all cats will respond to pheromone products, and it may take some time before any effects become evident.

Seeking Professional Help

In some cases, managing territorial behavior may necessitate professional assistance. A veterinarian behaviorist or animal behaviorist can assess your cat's behavior and craft a management plan tailored to each individual's needs.

Conclusion

Understanding and managing cat territorial behavior is an integral part of cat care that can promote peace and harmony in your home. By understanding your cat's territory, introducing new cats gradually, providing vertical space, using pheromone products, or seeking professional assistance if necessary, you can help manage territorial behavior while creating a tranquil environment for your feline friend.

Remember each cat is unique so take time to get to know them individually; with patience, understanding, and attention you'll develop a strong bond with your furry friend while managing their behavior accordingly - for both of you!

Dealing with Cat Anxiety

Cats, just like humans, can experience anxiety. This anxiety may take the form of hiding and avoiding social interaction to destructive behavior and excessive grooming. In this chapter, we'll look at some effective methods for dealing with cat anxiety and creating a calm environment for your furry friend.

Acknowledging Anxiety in Cats

Acknowledging anxiety in cats can be tricky due to their notorious ability to hide feelings. Nonetheless, there are some telltale signs that your feline friend may be feeling anxious:

Hiding

Avoiding social interaction

Excessive grooming

Destructive behavior

Excessive meowing or vocalization

Refusing food or water

If you believe your cat may be suffering from anxiety, consult a veterinarian to rule out any underlying medical conditions.

Reducing Stressors

Making changes in your cat's environment can help alleviate anxiety. Common stressors include changes to their routine, new people or animals in the home, loud noises, and other sources of discomfort.

Giving your cat a safe and secure space that they can call their own can help reduce anxiety. This may include providing them with a cozy bed, hiding spot, and scratching post for added stimulation.

Calming Products

Calming products such as pheromone sprays and diffusers can help reduce anxiety in cats. These solutions release relaxing pheromones which reduce stress and promote relaxation in cats.

It's essential to remember that not all cats will respond to calming products, and it may take some time before you see results.

Establishing a Routine

For your cat, creating a routine can help reduce anxiety. Cats thrive on predictability and consistency; providing them with regular feeding times, playtimes, and other activities helps ease stress and promote relaxation.

Establishing a routine can also help your cat feel secure and stable in their environment.

Seeking Professional Help

In some cases, dealing with cat anxiety may necessitate professional assistance. A veterinary behaviorist or animal behaviorist can assess your cat's behavior and create a management plan tailored to each individual's requirements.

Conclusion

Dealing with cat anxiety can be a challenging issue, but there are effective ways to create a calm and relaxed environment for your furry friend. By recognizing when your feline friend experiences anxiety, reducing stressors, using calming products, creating an organized routine, or seeking professional assistance if needed, you can help alleviate that feeling and promote a happy and healthy life for them. Remember each cat is unique so take time to get to know them on an individual level - with patience, understanding, and attention you can build a strong bond with each other while managing anxiety effectively for both of you.

Indoor vs. Outdoor Cats

One of the decisions cat owners must make is whether to keep their cats indoors or give them outdoor access. While both options have pros and cons, it's essential that you consider your cat's safety, health, and happiness when making this choice. In this chapter we'll look into both options in detail, providing tips for keeping your furry friend secure and contented.

Indoor Cats Have Pros and Cons

Indoor cats are protected from many of the hazards found outdoors, such as traffic, predators, and diseases. Furthermore, they're less likely to get lost or stolen.

Indoor cats tend to have a lower risk of injury or death and may live longer than outdoor cats. Furthermore, they tend not to engage in behaviors such as fighting, spraying, and marking territory.

Indoor cats may be at greater risk for obesity and other health issues if they don't receive enough exercise and mental stimulation. They could also become bored or develop behavior issues if they lack toys or playtime to engage in.

Pros and Cons of Outdoor Cats

Outdoor cats enjoy the benefits of fresh air, natural sunlight, and an engaging environment. Furthermore, these felines can engage in natural behaviors like hunting and climbing which can benefit their physical and mental well-being.

Outdoor cats are vulnerable to a range of hazards, including traffic, predators, disease exposure, and loss or theft. Outdoor cats may also engage in behaviors such as fighting, spraying, and marking territory.

Maintaining Your Cat's Safety and Happiness

Are you looking to keep your furry friend comfortable? Below are some tips to keep them secure and contented.

No matter if you choose to keep your cat indoors or give them outdoor access, it is essential that you take steps to keep them safe and content.

If you opt to keep your cat indoors, make sure they have plenty of toys, scratching posts, and playtime to stimulate both physical and mental stimulation. Most importantly, create a secure and comfortable environment where they can feel safe and secure in their own space.

When allowing your cat outdoor access, it is essential that they have a secure environment. This could include creating an enclosed catio or providing them with safe and secure outdoor space.

No matter if your cat lives indoors or outdoors, it is essential to provide them with regular veterinary care and monitor their health and behavior for any signs of illness or injury.

Conclusion

Ultimately, the decision to keep your cat indoors or allow them outdoor access should be based on your cat's safety, health, and happiness. By carefully considering both pros and cons of indoor and outdoor cats as well as taking steps to keep them secure and contented, you can help promote a happy and healthy life for your furry friend. Remember that each cat is unique so take time to get to know each one individually; with patience, understanding, and devotion you can build an intimate bond with your furry friend while making decisions that benefit both of you both.

Introducing Your Cat to Other Pets

Introducing your cat to other pets can be a challenging but also rewarding process. With patience, understanding, and love you can help your cat adjust and form an intimate bond with its new friend. In this chapter, we'll look at some of the most effective methods for introducing your cat to other pets while creating a harmonious environment at home.

Understanding Your Cat's Personality

Knowing your cat's personality is essential for successful communication between both of you.

Understanding your cat's personality is essential when introducing them to other pets. Some cats tend to be more social and outgoing than others, which may make them adapt faster to a new pet; on the other hand, some may require more effort and time for adjustment.

When introducing your cat to a new pet, it is essential to consider its individual personality.

Introduce Your Cat to a Dog: Are You Prepared?

Introducing your cat to a dog can be difficult, as their personalities and communication styles differ. Therefore, it is essential that you introduce the two creatures gradually, providing them with a secure environment in which to interact.

When introducing your cat to a dog, it's essential that they remain separate at first, allowing them to get familiar with each other's scent before meeting face-to-face. Furthermore, supervise their interactions and provide them with separate food, water, and litter boxes for each.

Introduce Your Cat to Another Cat

Introducing your cat to another cat can be a challenging endeavor, as cats tend to be territorial and may display aggressive behavior toward other felines. Therefore, it is best to introduce them slowly and gradually, providing them with a secure environment in which to interact.

When introducing your cat to another cat, it's essential that they remain separated initially. This allows them to become acquainted with each other's scent before meeting face-to-face. Furthermore, you should supervise their interactions and provide each cat with its own food, water, and litter box.

Offering Your Pet Their Own Space

Giving each pet its own space is essential for providing them with a secure, comforting atmosphere.

Establishing a separate space for each pet in your home is essential to creating harmony in the household. Each pet should have its own food, water, and litter boxes as well as a secure and comfortable area to retreat to when they require privacy.

Additionally, providing each pet with its own toys and playtime helps prevent territorial disputes and promotes mental and physical well-being.

Seeking Professional Help

In some cases, introducing your cat to other pets may necessitate professional assistance. A veterinarian behaviorist or animal behaviorist can assess your cat's behavior and create a management plan tailored to each individual's requirements.

Conclusion

Adopting a new pet can be daunting, but with patience, understanding, and love you can help your cat adjust. By understanding your cat's personality and introducing each pet gradually, providing each with its own space, and seeking professional assistance if needed, you can foster harmony in your home. Remember: each animal is unique so take time to get to know both of your furry friends on an individual level; with patience, understanding, and love from you all around, everyone will benefit from an enriching environment.

Nutrition and Feline Behavior

Nutrition is an integral part of your cat's overall health and well-being. Not only does it promote physical well-being, but the food you give them can also have an effect on their behavior and mental well-being too. In this chapter, we'll look into the significance of nutrition in feline behavior as well as offer helpful tips for selecting suitable food items for your furry friend.

Nutrition's Influence on Feline Behavior

What role does nutrition play in your cat's behavior?

Nutrition plays an integral role in feline behavior. What you feed your cat affects its energy levels, mood, and behavior. A diet high in protein and low in carbohydrates will help maintain stable blood sugar levels, reduce mood swings, and soothe behavioral issues.

Additionally, certain nutrients like omega-3 fatty acids have been known to promote mental well-being and reduce stress and anxiety in cats.

Selecting the Best Food for Your Feline Friend

Finding the ideal food for your pet can be daunting when you don't know where to begin when selecting what's best for them.

When selecting food for your feline friend, it's essential to take into account their individual nutritional requirements and preferences. Cats are carnivores, meaning they require a diet high in protein and low in carbohydrates.

When selecting cat food, it's essential to select one with superior protein sources like chicken, turkey, or fish. Look for foods low in carbohydrates and free from artificial preservatives and fillers.

Additionally, when selecting your cat's food, you should take into account their age, weight, and any medical conditions they may have.

Feeding Your Cat a Balanced Diet

Making sure your cat receives an optimal diet is important.

Feeding your cat a balanced diet is essential for their overall health and well-being. In addition to providing high-quality protein sources, make sure the diet contains essential vitamins, minerals, and nutrients that promote good health.

Offering your cat a variety of foods, such as wet and dry food, can help ensure they get a balanced diet. Additionally, monitoring your cat's weight and adjusting its food intake accordingly is important to prevent obesity or other health issues.

Conclusion

Nutrition plays an integral role in feline behavior and overall health. By selecting high-quality cat food that's high in protein and low in carbohydrates, providing essential vitamins and nutrients, and monitoring your cat's weight and food intake, you can promote a happy and healthy life for your furry friend. Remember each cat is unique; take time to get to know their individual nutritional needs and preferences. With patience, love, and care you can foster an intimate bond with your feline friend while providing them with the essential nutrition they need to thrive.

Cat Breeds and Personalities

Cats come in a wide variety of breeds, each with their own individual characteristics and personalities. Whether you're searching for an energetic feline friend or one that prefers to relax and cuddle, there is sure to be a breed out there that meets your needs. In this chapter, we'll take a closer look at some popular cat breeds and their personalities so you can find the ideal feline companion that complements your lifestyle.

Siamese Cats

Siamese cats are characterized by their dark points on faces, ears, paws, and tails. They also possess an outgoing nature with strong vocalizations. Furthermore, these intelligent felines love to play; making them ideal for families with children or active lifestyles.

Persian Cats

Persian cats are renowned for their long, luxurious coats and laid-back personalities. They exhibit affectionate kindness that makes them ideal for families with children or seniors looking for a companion that will take time out of the day to spend quality time together.

Sphynx Cats

Sphynx cats are renowned for their hairlessness and affectionate personalities. These outgoing cats enjoy cuddling with owners, making them an ideal choice for families searching for a lap cat.

Maine Coon Cats

Maine Coon cats are renowned for their large size and sweet personalities. They enjoy playing and interacting with humans, making them an ideal choice for families with children or seniors looking for a loyal, affectionate pet.

Bengal Cats

Bengal cats are highly energetic and active breeds, known for their wild-looking coat and energetic personalities. Intelligent and eager to play, Bengal cats make excellent companions for families with children or active lifestyles.

Ragdoll Cats

Ragdoll cats are beloved for their sweet personalities and gentle demeanor. They tend to be docile and love cuddling, making them an ideal choice for families with young children or seniors looking for a cuddly companion.

Senior Cat Care

As our cat's age, their care needs change and it is essential to adjust our routines accordingly. Senior cats require extra consideration when it comes to health, diet, and living environment; in this chapter, we'll cover some of the best practices in senior cat care as well as provide tips for creating a comfortable and fulfilling life for your aging feline friend.

Healthcare for Senior Cats

Regular veterinary care is essential for all cats, but it becomes even more essential as they age. Senior cats should visit the veterinarian at least twice annually for a comprehensive check-up and any necessary vaccinations.

It's essential to closely monitor your senior cat's health and seek veterinary help if you notice any changes in its behavior or condition.

Diet and Nutrition for Senior Cats

Are your senior pets on a special diet or nutrition plan? If so, here is some helpful information.

Cats' nutritional needs evolve as they age. Senior cats require a diet low in calories and fat to prevent obesity and other health problems. Furthermore, senior cats require more protein as well as certain vitamins and minerals to support their aging bodies.

It is essential to select high-quality senior cat food specifically tailored to the nutritional needs of older cats. You may also want to supplement your diet with supplements like omega-3 fatty acids for added support of joint health and mental well-being.

Senior Cats Need a Comfortable Living Environment

What kind of environment would you provide for senior cats to help them age gracefully?

Senior cats require a secure and comfortable living environment to ensure they remain contented and healthy. It's essential that you provide your senior cat with a cozy bed as well as plenty of soft blankets to cushion its aging joints.

You might also provide your senior cat with stairs or ramps to enable them to climb onto furniture or reach its favorite window perch.

Senior cats often benefit from a more peaceful and serene living environment. To ensure your senior cat feels secure and contented, it is important to minimize stressors such as loud noises or frequent visitors.

Exercise and Mental Stimulation for Senior Cats

Senior cats require physical and mental stimulation to keep their physical and mental well-being. It's essential that the activities chosen are suitable for their age and physical condition.

Gentle playtime for your senior cat, such as chasing a toy or engaging with a puzzle feeder, can help promote exercise and mental stimulation.

Conclusion

Senior cats require special consideration and care to ensure they lead a happy and healthy life. By providing your senior cat with regular veterinary services, a nutritious diet, a comfortable living environment, suitable exercise, and mental stimulation, you can promote an enriching quality of life for your aging furry friend. Remember each senior cat is unique; take time to get to know their individual needs and preferences by providing patience, love, and affection over time. With these steps taken towards senior cat care, you can build a strong bond with your furry friend that allows both of you to thrive!

Maintaining Good Behavior

Maintaining good behavior in your cat is essential for its health and happiness, as well as the peace and harmony of your home. With patience, consistency, and positive reinforcement you can help your feline friend maintain good manners and avoid problem behaviors. In this chapter, we'll look at some of the best practices to foster good behavior in cats.

Consistency in Training

Consistency is key when it comes to maintaining your cat's good behavior. Cats thrive off routine and predictability, so consistent training and reinforcement are highly successful at motivating them.

Establish clear rules and boundaries for your cat, then be consistent in upholding them. This could include placing limits on where they can go inside the house, teaching them to use a scratching post, as well as having an established feeding and playtime routine.

Positive Reinforcement

Positive reinforcement is an incredibly successful training technique that can help maintain good behavior in your cat. This involves rewarding them for good behaviors such as using the litter box or scratching posts with treats, toys, or praise.

It is essential to avoid punishing your cat for negative behaviors, such as scratching furniture or jumping on the counter. Instead, redirect their energy towards more appropriate outlets like a scratching post or cat tree.

Adequate Exercise and Stimulation

Cats need exercise and mental stimulation to promote good behavior and prevent problem behaviors. It is essential that you provide your cat with plenty of opportunities for play and physical activity, such as chasing toys or climbing a cat tree.

You can also provide your cat with mental stimulation by offering puzzle feeders, hiding treats around the house, and playing with interactive toys.

Minimizing Stressors

Stress can be a major contributor to problem behaviors in cats. To ensure your feline friend remains calm and relaxed, it's essential that you reduce any possible sources of stress in their environment.

By creating a peaceful living environment for your cat, they can reduce exposure to loud noises or unfamiliar people or animals while having a secure place where they can retreat when needed for privacy.

Conclusion

Maintaining good behavior in your cat is an integral part of promoting their health and happiness, as well as the harmony of your home. By consistent training, using positive reinforcement, providing adequate exercise and stimulation, and minimizing stressors, you can help your feline friend maintain good behavior and avoid problem behaviors. Remember each cat is unique; take time to get acquainted with their individual needs and preferences through patience, attention, and love. With these nurturing elements provided to them through patience and attention, fostering a strong bond will develop between both of you so they receive all that love they need to thrive.

www.ingramcontent.com/pod-product-compliance
Lightning Source LLC
Chambersburg PA
CBHW071127130526
44590CB00056B/2909